Who Were
The Three Stooges?

Who Were
The Three Stooges?

by Pam Pollack and Meg Belviso

illustrated by Ted Hammond

Grosset & Dunlap
An Imprint of Penguin Random House

To Raymond Pollack and Richard Pollack,
the Best of Brothers—PP

To the Sheehans, who share all the best qualities
of stooges—MB

To Doug—TH

GROSSET & DUNLAP
Penguin Young Readers Group
An Imprint of Penguin Random House LLC

Text copyright © 2016 by Pam Pollack and Meg Belviso. Illustrations copyright © 2016 by Penguin Random House LLC. All rights reserved. Published by Grosset & Dunlap, an imprint of Penguin Random House LLC, 345 Hudson Street, New York, New York 10014. Who HQ™ and all related logos are trademarks owned by Penguin Random House LLC. GROSSET & DUNLAP is a trademark of Penguin Random House LLC. Printed in the USA.

Library of Congress Cataloging-in-Publication Data is available.

ISBN 9780448488660 (paperback)   10 9 8 7 6 5 4 3 2 1
ISBN 9780399542442 (library binding)   10 9 8 7 6 5 4 3 2 1

Contents

Who Were the Three Stooges?

On September 28, 1934, a new film premiered at the Carthay Circle Theatre in Los Angeles. It was only eighteen minutes long—short enough to be shown before the main feature.

The movie was called *Men in Black* and it had three unusual stars. Their names were Moe Howard, Larry Fine, and Curly Howard. Together they were called the Three Stooges. They were a strange-looking trio. Moe had straight black hair that sat like an upside-down bowl on top of his head. Larry's frizzy hair stuck out on all sides. Curly had a head like a cue ball— he had no hair at all!

Moe had a tough face like a gangster that he scrunched up when he made a fist and barked things like, "Why, I oughta . . ."

Larry jumped whenever he was frightened.

Curly ran around in circles—sometimes even while lying on the floor, like a human pinwheel. He made funny sounds—"Nyuk nyuk nyuk!" and "Woo woo woo woo!" When he spoke he had a high, squeaky voice. "Soitenly!" Curly said in his thick Brooklyn accent when he was sure about something. "I'm just a victim of soi-cumstance!" he said when he wasn't.

In the movie, Moe, Larry, and Curly played doctors—but they didn't cure many patients. They rode bicycles, horses, and tiny cars through the halls of the hospital. They broke windows and knocked people over the head with mallets. Mostly they fought with one another.

"Why, I oughta . . . !" Moe growled before slapping Curly on the head and poking him in the eye. Larry shrieked as Moe pulled him by the hair. "Nyuk nyuk nyuk!" Curly said. Then he ran down the hall, hooting, "Woo woo woo woo woo woo woo!"

None of the Three Stooges were hurt in their fights. It was all part of their comedy act. The three men would do anything for a laugh. And the audience loved it.

Men in Black was the official movie debut of the Three Stooges. But the three men had known one another for years. Curly was Moe's little brother. Larry was practically part of the family, too. They would go through good times and bad in their lives, but they always stuck together. They were closer than brothers—they were Stooges!

CHAPTER 1
A Brooklyn Beginning

In 1897, Brooklyn, New York, was a city full of immigrants—people who had come from other countries to make a new life in America. Jennie and Solomon Horwitz had traveled by boat from Lithuania to New York City.

Immigrants in the United States

Between 1815 and 1915, about thirty million people arrived in the United States from many European countries, including Italy, Ireland, and Poland. It was not an easy trip. Many people traveled miles on foot or by river to get to a steamship in their home port that would bring them to the United States. They then spent weeks on overcrowded boats.

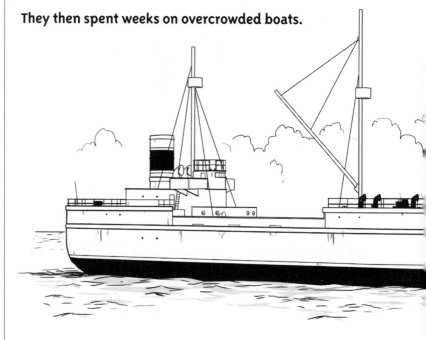

Many immigrants were escaping poverty. Some were looking for religious freedom. All hoped to start better lives in America.

By the beginning of the twentieth century, immigrants made up more than 40 percent of the population of New York City.

When Sol wasn't working in a clothing factory, he spent as much time as he could at the local synagogue, studying the Jewish holy books and praying. Jennie was a woman ahead of her time. She made most of the money for the family, renting out rooms and later becoming a successful real estate agent.

When Moses Harry Horwitz was born on June 19, 1897, he already had three older brothers: Irving, Benjamin (known as Jack), and Sam.

Sam, who was two years older than Moses, was always known as Shemp because of the way his mother pronounced his name in her Lithuanian accent. Moses quickly became known as Moe.

Jack and Irving were well-behaved children. Shemp was the clown of the family. In school he was always getting in trouble for making funny faces and drawing pictures. His mother was constantly getting called to the school to talk to Shemp's teachers about his behavior. She spent so much time there that when Shemp graduated from sixth grade, the principal announced (as he gave Shemp his diploma) that "This young man did not graduate . . . his mother did."

Shemp's little brother Moe had his own problems in school: bullies. As a little boy Moe had long hair that fell in fat curls to his shoulders. His mother loved getting up early to curl his hair for school.

The other kids thought Moe's hair made him look funny. Both boys and girls teased him. Not a day went by when he didn't get into a fight. Even the principal called him the "student with the beautiful hair."

Moe never told his mother about the fights. He knew how much she loved his hair, and he loved her.

On October 22, 1903, when Moe was six, Jennie had another son. His name was Jerome. Moe nicknamed him Babe. Shemp and Moe were thrilled to have a new brother. Not long after he was born, they took him out for a walk in his baby carriage.

To make the ride more fun for the new baby, they took the carriage to the top of a hill and prepared to let it go down at full speed. Luckily, their parents arrived just in time to stop the wild ride.

At school, Moe was still fighting off bullies on his own. One day when he was eleven, a boy began to pick on him. Another boy jumped in and punched the bully in the nose. He made him apologize to Moe.

After school Moe went over to his new friend's house. The boy's bedroom was full of pictures of boxers and boxing equipment. Moe looked at himself in the mirror. His new friend looked like an ordinary boy. But Moe still had long curls. At that moment Moe made a decision. He picked up a pair of scissors from the dresser. With his eyes closed, he clipped off his curls one by one. When he opened his eyes again the curls were lying on the floor. Moe's hair was flat against his head, the ends crudely chopped. He wasn't going to be bullied anymore.

CHAPTER 2
The Good Ship *Sunflower*

Even though he was no longer being teased, Moe still didn't like school. By the time he was eleven, he already knew what he wanted to be when he grew up: an actor. During the spring of 1908, Moe attended school only 40 days out of 103. When the school sent letters home telling his parents about his absences, Moe stole them from the mailbox.

He went so far as to write a note to the school saying that he was attending a different school closer to his grandmother's house—even though both of his grandmothers lived in Lithuania!

Instead of going to classes, Moe spent his days going to theaters to see plays. He would pick out one actor to focus on during the show. He watched the whole play as if *he* was that actor. In bed that night, he repeated all the lines he could remember from the play.

In May 1909, Moe went to the Vitagraph Studio in Brooklyn. He asked if there were any jobs at the movie studio for a young boy. Soon Moe was running errands.

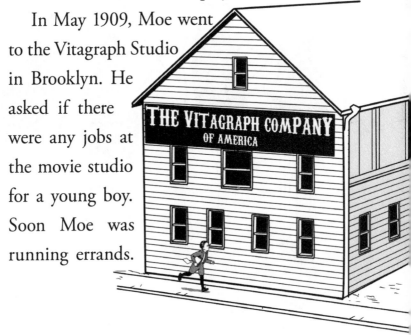

He refused any payment for his work at Vitagraph—until he was cast as a background performer in the short, silent movies the studio made. In his first movie he played a bully who pushed other kids around. And he got paid for it.

On July 3 that same year, Moe met a new friend on the beach at Coney Island in Brooklyn. His name was Lee Nash. The two became best friends. In 1912, when they were fifteen, they joined the Annette Kellerman Diving Girls.

The group of ten girls dove off a thirty-foot diving board into a tank of water. If the audience on the boardwalk looked closely at four of those ten "girls" they might notice that they were actually boys, including Moe and Lee!

Moe was still very close to his brother Shemp. And Shemp was a good performer himself. He played the ukulele at parties and acted out comedy routines. In 1914, Shemp told Moe that he had a friend who would write the two of them a comedy act they could perform onstage. Moe agreed to do the act, but secretly he had already applied for a different job.

He had answered an ad in the newspaper for a young actor to perform in plays for tourists on a showboat named *Sunflower*, sailed by Captain Billy Bryson. The boat was docked in Jackson, Mississippi.

Moe really wanted the job, but he had to send a photograph of himself along with the application. Moe had no pictures of himself. And he couldn't afford to have them taken. What could he do? He looked up at the wall above his head. There hung a photograph of a neighbor who happened to be tall, dark, and handsome. Moe thought he was perfect! He took the picture off the wall and sent it to Captain Billy. Weeks later Moe got a package with train fare for Mississippi.

Shemp was upset when he learned they would not be doing their act. He thought what Moe had done was crazy. But he put his arm around his brother and wished him well.

Moe left for Mississippi and his first big acting job. When Captain Billy got a look at him, he was furious. This was not the handsome man in the picture! "How could anyone pull a stunt like this?" the captain shouted.

Moe pleaded with Captain Billy not to send him home. So Moe was given a job cleaning the theater and the dressing rooms. His salary all went to Captain Billy to pay him back for the train fare.

But Moe didn't give up on his dream of acting. He asked Captain Billy to give him a role in one of the plays on the ship. "I'm going to be an actor—a very good one," Moe told him.

Captain Billy said that from what he'd seen of Moe so far, he believed he could be anything he set out to be. Moe got the part—

and more parts after that. Soon Moe was performing regularly on the *Sunflower*. He got a raise in his salary—and he got to keep the money.

Moe worked on the *Sunflower* for two summers, playing all kinds of parts. He was ready to return to New York and find work on the stage. This time he would do it with Shemp by his side.

CHAPTER 3
Cleanup Act

Moe and Shemp worked out an act where they would sing songs and tell jokes. To work in the theater they first had to have an agent—someone who would find jobs and get them hired. For weeks they visited one agency after another. Everyone turned them down. Finally one man said yes. He got Moe and Shemp a job at the Mystic Theater in New York City. When their new agent asked them their stage names, they changed their names to Howard & Howard because they thought that sounded more American than Horwitz & Horwitz. For the rest of their lives they were the Howard brothers.

Vaudeville

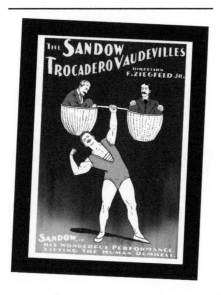

From the 1880s to the early 1930s, the most popular entertainment in the United States was vaudeville. People would go to the theater to see a series of different acts on the same stage, one after another. They might see a singer followed by a dancer, a juggler, acrobats, or trained animals. One of the most popular kinds of acts were comedians who told jokes and sang funny songs.

When it was time for Moe and Shemp to go onstage, the owner of the theater would yell, "Howard and Howard, up and at 'em!" The boys jumped onstage. Nobody in the audience applauded. So they tried some jokes. Nobody laughed. In fact, most of the audience got up to leave!

After a few performances Moe and Shemp realized that they had been hired as the "cleanup" act. That meant that the theater owner thought they were so bad they would drive the audience away. By the time Howard & Howard's act was over, the theater could be cleaned up before the next show.

Despite their rough start, Moe and Shemp kept working. They performed six shows on Friday, nine shows on Saturday, and eight on Sunday! They learned more jokes and songs. Some of the theaters where they worked weren't very nice. Their dressing rooms were cold and drafty.

Sometimes they didn't even have dressing rooms. They changed in storage rooms filled with big bags of popcorn and occasionally even rats!

One day in the winter of 1922, Moe saw a newspaper ad for a vaudeville act called Ted and Betty Healy. He went to see the act. It turned out that Moe's childhood friend, Lee Nash, had adopted the stage name Ted Healy! Lee, who now was called Ted by everyone, was thrilled to see his old friend again. He gave Moe a job performing with him, his wife, Betty, and their dog, Pete.

Ted and Betty Healy

One night during the act, Ted and Moe heard a familiar laugh in the audience. It was Shemp. Ted would often call up someone from the audience to joke around with onstage. This time he asked Shemp. Shemp came up, eating a pear. He offered a bite to Ted, and Ted refused. Shemp insisted, so Ted smashed it into his face.

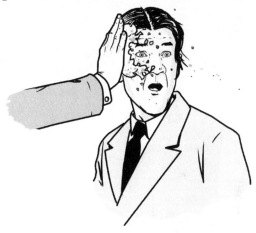

The two got into a pretend fight. The audience roared. From then on Shemp was part of the act, too. They performed under many names, including Ted Healy and His Gang and Ted Healy and His Racketeers.

Ted described the parts that Moe and Shemp played in his act as "stooges." A stooge, according to Ted, was a guy who you could really push around. "Whenever I'm in doubt or feel mixed up, I always hit the nearest stooge," he explained. Of course, Ted wasn't really hitting Moe and Shemp. He was just pretending to be angry enough to bop them over the head, tweak their noses, or throw things at them. Even when they were the butt of the joke, the audience was always on the stooges' side. They were the ones getting all the laughs.

Moe and Shemp were gaining a lot of fans. And no one was a bigger fan than their younger brother, Babe. He went to as many of their shows as he could, studying their act. Secretly, he wished he could join his brothers onstage.

The brothers were making enough money to think about settling down. Coincidentally, they each married their Brooklyn girlfriends in 1925.

Shemp married Gertrude Frank. Moe married
Helen Schonberger. Moe thought he should leave

show business and get a more stable job, especially after his daughter, Joan, was born. Although Moe thought he was doing the right thing, the vaudeville stage was his true calling.

CHAPTER 4
Larry

While Moe was attempting to become a more serious family man, Shemp kept performing with Ted Healy. When Shemp got an offer to join another show, he didn't want to leave Ted without finding someone to replace him. In Chicago, Shemp found just the right person. He was a young man with curly hair who wore a silk top hat and a tuxedo. He played the violin. From the waist up, he looked like a serious violinist—but his legs were doing a crazy Russian dance, bouncing up and down and kicking out in all directions.

Shemp knew a stooge when he saw one, and this was a stooge.

The man with the violin was Larry Fine.

He was born Larry Feinberg and had grown up in Philadelphia, about a hundred miles away from the Howards in Brooklyn. He started playing the violin after he had an accident at his father's jewelry shop when he was four. Larry burned his hand and arm badly. The doctor thought playing the violin would help it grow stronger.

Like Moe and Shemp, Larry longed to be in show business. He'd started performing in comedy acts when he was fourteen. By the time he met Shemp, Larry was already married to his wife,

Larry and Mabel Fine

Mabel. Ted suggested that Larry stand backstage to observe the act. Larry did not know that Ted planned to shove him onstage during the show.

Suddenly he found himself in front of the audience with no idea what was going to happen. So Larry did what he did best: he made the audience laugh.

He pretended to be even more nervous and frightened than he was. He let Ted push him around. The audience loved him. He was in!

After they finished their shows in Chicago, Larry went back to his favorite town, Atlantic City, in New Jersey. His wife, Mabel, had good news: They were going to have a baby. Soon after Larry's daughter, Phyllis, was born, he got a call from Ted. Ted said had an idea for a new act. Ted now wanted *three* stooges onstage with him. Shemp had already agreed, and so had Moe. Would Larry join them? Of course!

The BIGGEST LAUGH IN NEW YORK

•

A NIGHT IN VENICE

•

TED HEALY *and his three Southern Gentlemen*

Ted tried out different names for his new act: Ted Healy and His Three Southern Gentlemen, Ted Healy and His Three Lost Souls, and even Ted Healy and His Three Stooges.

Moe, Larry, and Shemp first started performing together in 1929. They got lots of practice being stooges. The longer they worked together, the better the act became. They traveled around the country performing at different theaters doing their act. They told jokes and did "slapstick" humor—gags that usually involved getting knocked around or falling down. The stooges did a lot of that.

Not only did Ted get to push them around and hit them with props, but—as part of the act—they pretended to annoy one another. Moe was especially good at faking a fight. In one of his most famous moves, Moe would pretend to poke another stooge in the eye. In reality he would touch them right under the eye with two fingers.

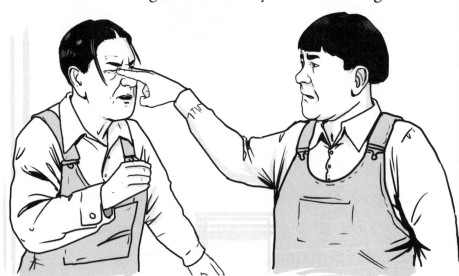

As long as Larry or Shemp stayed perfectly still, they knew Moe would never hurt them. Even though Moe's act was to bully them, Shemp and Larry trusted him more than anyone.

There was one person who felt left out of all the excitement: Babe. All his life he'd looked up to his older brothers. He had always wanted to be part of their jokes. He had spent hours cheering them on from the audience. Then, in 1928, Babe got his own lucky break.

He got a job as the orchestra leader for Orville Knapp's band. But he didn't know how to conduct an orchestra. He didn't have to. In the act, he pretended to conduct the musicians while—little by little—his clothes fell apart! First his coat split up the back. Then his pants tore in two, revealing the long underwear he wore held together across his bottom by a giant safety pin. Babe was becoming a real stooge.

CHAPTER 5
Curly

SOUP TO NUTS

Starring Ted Healy and his Racketeers

In 1929, Hollywood became interested in Ted Healy and His Three Stooges. They all went out to California to make a short film called *Soup to Nuts*. Ted was the star. But when the film came out, the stooges got all the attention—even though Moe, Larry, and Shemp were not yet known as anything other than part of Ted's act. Moe, Larry, and Shemp were all offered contracts by a big movie studio.

Ted was not. But he wasn't about to let the three men who played stooges in his act become stars without him. He convinced the studio to cancel their offer.

Moe, Shemp, and Larry were angry with Ted and began to perform on the road without him, usually billed as Howard, Fine, & Howard. They realized that Ted wasn't a very good friend. Still, when Ted asked them to rejoin him in 1932, they did; Ted was still a big star on the stage, and they weren't. Shemp, however, didn't want to work with Ted anymore. When he was asked to be in a film, he left the act to do it.

"Healy asked me who's going to replace Shemp," Moe said to his brother, Babe, over the phone. "I told him I'd call my brother, Jerome."

Jerome? That was him! Moe set up an audition with Ted. When Babe got to the theater, he was nervous. He didn't have a lot of experience. Moe was nervous, too—he knew how much his little brother wanted the job. Ted didn't think Babe was a good fit. He looked too normal. Moe was known for his thick black bowl-shaped haircut. Onstage Larry fluffed up his curly hair so it would stick straight up. Babe's hair was thick and wavy. He looked too normal to be a stooge. "Maybe you should shave your head," Ted suggested.

In 1932, it wasn't very common for a man to shave his head. It seemed like a ridiculous idea! But it was Babe's dream to be a stooge.

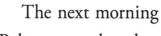

The next morning Babe returned to the theater. He walked lightly down the aisle onto the stage. There, he took off his cap with a flourish. Moe, Larry, and Ted stared at his bald head in shock. "Call me Curly," Jerome said, making a joke about his bald head. The name stuck.

Finally, Ted found the right words: "You're in."

For his first few shows all Curly did was run back and forth on the stage wearing a bathing suit and carrying a tiny bucket of water. When his nervousness made him speak in a high, squeaky voice, he worked it into the act.

When he forgot his lines—which was often—
he made funny noises that kept the audience
laughing. Sometimes he dropped to the floor
and spun around on his side. Everyone quickly
realized that Curly was something special.

Funny Brothers

Moe, Shemp, and Curly Howard weren't the only brothers to become comedy stars. Some other famous brother comedy teams were

The Marx Brothers

Julius, Leonard, and Adolph were the real names of Groucho, Chico, and Harpo Marx. They grew up in New York City around the same time as the Stooges. All talented musicians as well as clowns, they got their start in vaudeville and went on to star in classic

Hollywood movies. Some of their most famous films include *Duck Soup*, *Monkey Business*, and *A Day at the Races*.

The Smothers Brothers

The Smothers brothers—Tom and Dick Smothers—were singers, musicians, and comedians. They were raised by their mother in the Los Angeles area after their father died in World War II. In the 1960s they had a popular TV show called *The Smothers Brothers Comedy Hour.*

In 1933, Ted Healy and His Three Stooges returned to Hollywood. They made five short movies, but Larry, Moe, and Curly really wanted to perform on their own. Moe convinced Ted that it would better for all of them if they went their separate ways. Ted agreed.

Moe quickly set out to get a contract for the Three Stooges. He arranged a meeting with a man from the Columbia movie studio.

The Three Stooges were offered a contract to do a movie with Columbia. If the studio liked the movie, they would do more. Moe signed the deal on behalf of himself, Larry, and Curly.

When he got back to his apartment, he met with Curly and Larry to tell them the good news. "Boys, we've accomplished what I was hoping for, a contract at Columbia!" he announced.

"A contract at Columbia?" said Larry. "I've just signed one at Universal!"

Larry had also made a deal on behalf of all the Stooges. The two studios checked in with each other to see who had signed their contract first. Columbia won.

The Stooges were no longer a part of someone else's act. They were striking out on their own.

CHAPTER 6
The Big Time

The first official "Three Stooges" movie was called *Men in Black*. It included a lot of jokes from their vaudeville act. Moe quickly began writing a new idea for another movie. The studio liked Moe's idea so much they offered the Three Stooges a new contract. It wasn't for one movie, but for eight short movies a year for twenty-five years!

The Movie before the Movie

In the early days of movies, beginning around 1920, audiences always saw a short film before the feature or main attraction. Many of these shorter

films ran about fifteen or twenty minutes and featured recurring characters. Some of the most popular characters were Our Gang, also known as the Little Rascals, Charlie Chaplin's Little Tramp, and of course, the Three Stooges.

In 1934, when *Men in Black* was shown in theaters, it was a big hit. In the movie, the Three Stooges play doctors handling a series of emergencies. They hurry to patients' rooms in go-karts, on a three-person bicycle, and even on horseback. The head of the hospital isn't pleased with their work—especially after they operate on *him* and accidentally leave all of their medical tools inside their patient. *Men in Black* was nominated for an Academy Award for Best Short Subject—Comedy.

The Stooges were now movie stars. Larry's mother was so proud she would stand up in movie theaters, point to the screen, and say, "That's my son!" when the movie played. Mrs. Horwitz wasn't so happy. She thought Moe and Curly looked and acted crazy on-screen!

Why couldn't they have sensible jobs *not* in show business, like Jack and Irving? Shemp, too, began appearing in movies on his own. Like his brothers, he was always the clown.

The Three Stooges continued to perform onstage as well as on-screen. At one show Larry's five-year-old niece was in the audience. When Moe started dragging Larry around the stage by the nose, the little girl started screaming,

"You're hurting my Uncle Larry!" Larry immediately stopped the act. He walked over to the little girl and assured her that it was only make-believe. "Are you really okay, Uncle Larry?" she asked.

"You bet," he said.

The audience clapped. They didn't mind the show being interrupted. They appreciated that family was important to the Stooges!

And their families were growing. Moe, Shemp, and Curly asked their parents to move to California so they could be together more often. Moe and Larry both had sons. Curly got married in 1937 and had a daughter named Marilyn.

Every place they went, the Stooges were recognized—they were hard to miss! Their faces and their crazy haircuts were everywhere. After the success of *Men in Black,* Columbia Studios made a deal to sell toys and other products based on their new comedy stars, including a set of hand puppets that looked just like the Stooges.

As promised, the Stooges made eight movies a year beginning in 1935. All of the Stooges' movies featured crazy stunts. They were often hit with hammers and covered with ants, mud, and cream pies. Audiences loved them in movies like *Three Little Pigskins* (where they played football players), *Pop Goes the Easel* (where they go to art school),

Ants in the Pantry (where they're exterminators), and *Goofs and Saddles* (where they join the cavalry in the Old West). *Slippery Silks* featured one of the biggest pie fights of all time. One hundred and fifty pies were thrown in that movie alone.

The Three Stooges were also becoming famous outside the United States. In 1939, they decided to tour internationally.

The Stooges were going to England.

CHAPTER 7
The Stooges Go to War

In July 1939, Larry, Moe, and Curly boarded a cruise ship, the *Queen Mary*, and sailed to England. The ship's captain was such a big fan, he gave the men first-class cabins even though they had only second-class tickets.

The Stooges arrived in London around the same time the queen of England was visiting the United States. The men laughed when they saw a newspaper headline that read "STOOGES ARRIVE IN LONDON—QUEEN LEAVES FOR AMERICA."

Larry, Moe, and Curly did their act for two weeks at the London Palladium theater. For the people in the audience, this was a chance to see their favorite movie stars in person. Because they had spent years performing live in theaters, the Stooges had no problem re-creating the stunts from their movies onstage. They were such a big hit in London that they were invited to other cities. They went to Blackpool, a summer resort town, and then on to Dublin, Ireland.

After Dublin they traveled to Glasgow, Scotland. Then they got offers to perform in dozens of other cities. But they were already scheduled to return to New York. As they

prepared to leave London, Larry, Moe, and Curly noticed that the city was making its own preparations. Bomb shelters were built in parks and fire drills were conducted often for the public. The English people thought they might soon be at war with Germany, but they didn't know when.

Back home the Stooges starred in a show called *George White's Scandals of 1939* in a theater in Times Square in New York City. Above the theater was an electric sign made to look like the Three Stooges. Moe liked to stand with the crowd on the street and watch as the Moe in the moving sign poked the other Stooges in the eye.

In September, the Howard family got sad news when their beloved mother, Jennie, died in California. Jennie had always been the center of the family. And now she was gone. The family was changing. The world was changing, too. A short time later, the war between England and Germany began. Other countries soon joined in the fight.

As the US Army, Navy, and Marines prepared to go to war, the Coca-Cola Company hired the Three Stooges to do a tour of military bases during their time off. Larry, Moe, and Curly were transported in a private air-conditioned bus from base to base. They performed one show

a night. Before the show, they were entertained by the commanding officers. They felt important, knowing they were doing their part to cheer up the troops.

Now back in California, all three men spent more time at home. Moe was proud of his victory garden—a backyard garden where he grew food for the family like potatoes, onions, green peppers,

and corn. During the war, the US government encouraged people to grow their own produce.

World War II

In 1939, Germany invaded the nearby country of Poland. Germany's leader at the time was Adolf Hitler. He believed that Germany should control all of Europe. The Axis Powers, led by Germany, Italy, and Japan, fought the Allied Powers, led by Great Britain, France, and the USSR. The United States joined the Allies on December 7, 1941, after Japan bombed Pearl Harbor, a US military base in Hawaii.

Adolf Hitler

Moe and Shemp also raised chickens. The whole family shared Moe's vegetables. They spent much of their time off together. And they happily celebrated the wedding of Moe's daughter, Joan, and later Larry's daughter, Phyllis.

The war ended in 1945. The Three Stooges were as popular as ever. But Moe and Larry began to worry about Curly. He had always had trouble remembering his lines, but lately it was becoming more of a problem. Sometimes Curly couldn't do simple things like put something in his mouth on camera. He was often confused. Curly went to a doctor who told him he needed more rest.

One day in May 1946, the three men were filming *Half-Wits Holiday*, their ninety-seventh short film for

The Stooges' latest SHE-nanigans!

The
THREE
STOOGES

CURLY   LARRY   MOE

Half-Wits Holiday

with
VERNON DENT   BARBARA SLATER   TED LORCH
Produced and Directed by JULES WHITE
A COLUMBIA SHORT-SUBJECT PRESENTATION

Columbia. Moe and Larry were together filming a scene. Curly sat nearby waiting to film his part. When they called Curly over, he didn't answer. Moe went over to his chair. "Babe?" said Moe, calling him by his old nickname.

Curly tried, but couldn't answer. It seemed as if he had fainted. But Curly had had a stroke—his brain wasn't getting the oxygen that it needed. Moe and Larry rushed Curly to the hospital, but he didn't recover in time to finish the movie.

CHAPTER 8
Changes

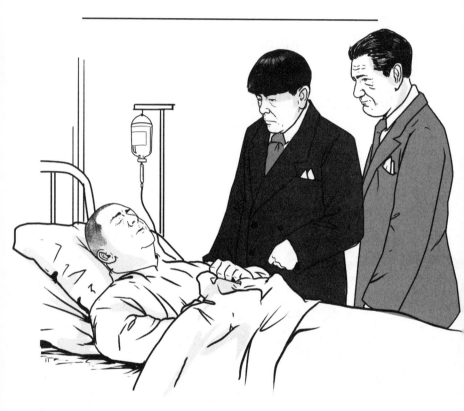

Curly's brothers Moe and Shemp were by his side every day as he slowly recovered from his stroke. It affected the way he moved and even spoke.

Curly could no longer make movies, but he could enjoy time with his family. In fact, Curly even fell in love again. He had been divorced when he met Valerie Newman. She and Curly were married in July 1947 and soon had a daughter named Jane.

Without Curly the team was a Stooge short. Who could replace him? There was only one answer: Shemp. He immediately stepped back into the act so the Three Stooges never missed making a movie in their contract. The first Three Stooges short with Shemp was *Fright Night*. Although Shemp was in many ways an original Stooge, when people thought of the Three Stooges they always thought of Moe, Larry, and Curly. When a Three Stooges comic book was published in 1949, it featured Moe, Larry, and Curly—even though by then Shemp had taken over. Shemp didn't mind, though. He was proud of his little brother.

Larry suggested that all three of them take part of their salaries and use it to help pay for Curly's medical bills. Moe and Shemp had long considered Larry to be like a brother. Now they knew that he cared about Curly as much as they did. Even though the Stooges were big movie stars, they weren't multimillionaires. Their salaries allowed them to live comfortable lives, but they made nowhere near what a movie star might earn today.

The Three Stooges worked very hard for the money they earned. Most years they made eight shorts with time off in the summer. During their vacations they almost always traveled to perform live shows in theaters around the country. Once the Stooges were the "cleanup" act that drove people away, and only backup players to Ted Healy. Now they were recognized all over the world. People imitated them. They said "Soitenly!" and "Why, I oughta . . . !" When the Stooges were growing up and dreaming of being onstage, none of them had ever imagined this kind of fame. They just wanted to make people laugh.

Curly did make one final appearance in a Three Stooges movie. In *Hold That Lion!* Moe, Larry, and Shemp find a snoring man on a train. The man is Curly. Some audience members might not have recognized him with his thick, wavy hair. But now that he was no longer a Stooge, Curly

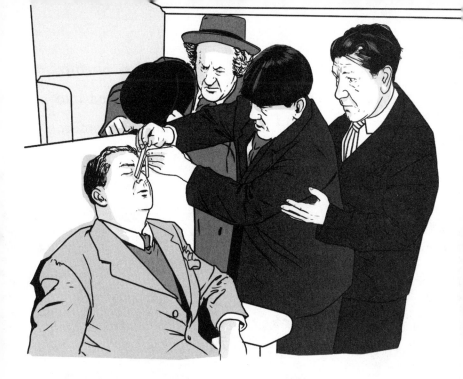

could finally grow his hair. This was the only movie in which all three of the acting Howard brothers—Moe, Shemp, and Curly—appeared together on-screen.

As much fun as it was to work with Shemp, everyone hoped that one day Curly would get well enough to return to the cast of the Stooges films. But on January 18, 1952, Curly had another stroke and died. He was forty-eight years old.

As sad as they were to lose Curly, Moe, Shemp, and Larry were still a family. And it looked like the Stooges would continue on for many more years. But one night in November 1955, Shemp went to see a boxing match with some friends.

After the fight, Shemp was laughing and telling jokes. Then he closed his eyes as if he was going to sleep. To his friends' shock, he had suddenly had a heart attack and died!

Moe and Larry were devastated. They didn't know how they could continue without Shemp.

They turned to a comedian friend named Joe Besser. Joe had been in movies and on television, too. They chose him as the new third Stooge and used his real name, Joe.

Moe and Larry worked with Joe Besser until their contract with Columbia ended in 1958. It had lasted twenty-five years. In that time, the

Three Stooges had made 190 short films. And some of them had yet to be released. It was hard for them to imagine not having to make movies every year. They weren't ready to retire. So the Stooges decided to do what they'd always done: perform onstage.

CHAPTER 9
Comeback

Joe Besser *was* ready to retire. He decided not to join Moe and Larry in their new stage show. Luckily they found their new third Stooge in a man named Joe DeRita. He would go by the name Curly Joe.

Joe Besser and Joe Derita

Joe Besser and Joe DeRita both had long acting careers in comedy before they became Stooges. Joe Besser grew up in Saint Louis, Missouri. He was in many films at Columbia Studios. He also appeared on early television playing a bratty character named Oswald "Stinky" Davis.

Joe DeRita was born in Philadelphia. His parents were vaudeville performers and he had acted with them even as a little boy. He was best known for being Curly Joe, the last Stooge.

Just as movies replaced vaudeville as the new popular entertainment, movies now had competition from television. Since the early 1950s, when there were only a few stations operating on the East and West coasts, television had grown in popularity. In 1953, less than half of all US households had TV sets, but by 1960, nine out of ten homes in the United States would have a television.

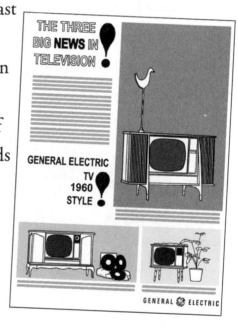

TV stations were eager to find programs to fill their time on the air. They loved to show old movies. For audiences, it was exciting to see movies they remembered from the big screen right in their own homes. Many of the old shorts, including cartoons, were popular with kids. In 1958, Columbia Studios released seventy-eight of the Three Stooges' films to their new television division. They were hoping to sell them to any television network that was interested in showing them. Many stations put the Three Stooges short films on in the afternoons.

The television programming executives didn't know it, but they'd just created a new phenomenon. Children ran home to see the Three Stooges after school. They had never seen these early films. They had not even been born when the brothers started making them. But they thought the Stooges were hilarious! Playgrounds were suddenly full of little girls and boys shouting "Nyuk nyuk nyuk!" and "Oh, a wise guy, eh?"

In the summer of 1958, the owner of a Pittsburgh nightclub was at home reading the newspaper. He couldn't concentrate because his kids were laughing so loudly. Finally he asked them what was so funny. They pointed to the Three Stooges on TV. The man immediately called the three men and asked if they wanted to perform at his theater in Pittsburgh for five days. They agreed.

When Moe, Larry, and Curly Joe entered the theater they were greeted with wild applause and

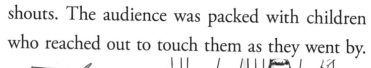

shouts. The audience was packed with children who reached out to touch them as they went by.

They decided to extend their stay in Pittsburgh and added three weeks' worth of shows. A local TV station held a contest for kids to make their own Three Stooges out of unusual things. They received over twenty-five thousand entries, including Stooges made out of hard-boiled eggs!

Suddenly the Three Stooges were bigger than ever. There were Three Stooges Halloween costumes, comic books, finger puppets, hats, T-shirts, and much more. Their new young fans wanted anything "Stooges" they could get their hands on.

Moe's son-in-law started the Three Stooges Fan Club out of his house. For fifty cents kids received a fan club ID card, a club certificate, photographs of the Stooges, and a personal letter. He got thousands of letters from kids who wanted to join. Some kids dropped fifty pennies into the envelope for their membership. Others taped, sewed, or glued their money to the letter, which made it hard to count! The fan club made over $22,000 in its first year—that was a lot of pennies!

The Three Stooges appeared in commercials for car wax, chocolates, and hair spray. They began getting offers to do full-length movies. *Have Rocket Will Travel*, a science-fiction comedy, was released in movie theaters in 1959, followed by *Snow White and the Three Stooges* and the *Three Stooges Meet Hercules*. Knowing that they were making these movies strictly for younger audiences now, the Stooges decided to make these films less violent. They sometimes got hit by accident, but they no longer slapped each other or poked each other in the eye. They did not want kids in the audience to copy them.

By the end of the 1960s, the Three Stooges were bigger stars than ever! They were making plans to do a TV show called *Kook's Tour*. The Stooges wanted to tour the world and get into trouble everywhere they went. They were excited about the project.

But on January 9, 1970, Larry, too, had a stroke. He could no longer walk and couldn't talk very well. Without Larry, Moe knew that the Stooges were truly over.

CHAPTER 10
Stooges Forever

Larry was too sick to ever work again. He moved into the Motion Picture Country House and Hospital, where he worked hard to recover. He still couldn't walk, but his speech got much better— good enough that he could sing and tell jokes in the annual "Ding-a-Ling Show," singing with other patients. Moe visited Larry all the time, and sometimes the two of them performed together.

Motion Picture Country House and Hospital

MOTION PICTURE AND TELEVISION HOSPITAL

The Motion Picture and Television Country House and Hospital is a retirement community for people in show business. Anyone who is over seventy and has worked steadily in film or television for at least twenty years can stay there. The hospital was opened in 1948. The ceremony to open the hospital on the grounds

was attended by Shirley Temple and also by Ronald Reagan, who later became president of the United States.

Not only did Curly and Larry live there, but Joe DeRita did, too, in later years.

After all, even though they were not related, they had been working and living as "brothers" for most of their lives.

Sometimes Larry visited local high schools to talk about his career. The kids who had loved watching the Three Stooges on television in the 1950s were now growing up and were thrilled to meet Larry in person.

Even though Larry remained quite active and had a great attitude, his health continued to decline. On January 25, 1975, Larry died quietly at the Motion Picture Country House. He was seventy-two years old.

Larry hadn't been the only Stooge who was still making people laugh long into his retirement. When Moe received an invitation to visit Salem College in West Virginia, he thought it was pretty funny because he had never even graduated high school! But he thought it would be a great experience to speak with the students there.

The college showed a couple of short Stooges films, and then Moe talked about what it was like to have been one of the Three Stooges. After his appearance at Salem College, Moe got invitations to speak at other schools. He was often greeted by packed auditoriums, sometimes with students filling the aisles as well as the seats.

Moe also appeared on TV talk shows.

During a visit to the *Mike Douglas Show* in 1975, Mike suggested that Moe bring his wife, Helen, onstage so that everyone could meet her. Moe went over to Helen in the audience and leaned over to help her up. In a very "Stooges" move, Helen pushed a pie right into Moe's face!

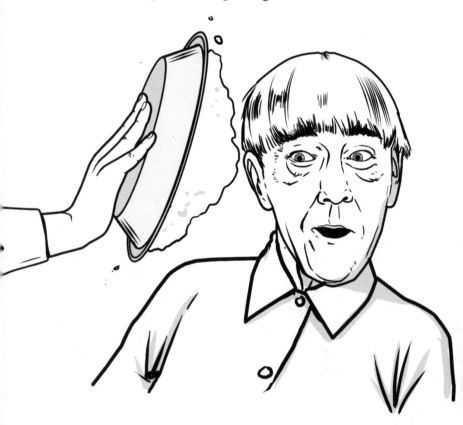

It was the first pie she'd ever thrown, and for Moe it was one of the high points of their life together. Moe died on May 4, 1975, just a few months before his beloved wife Helen.

The Three Stooges have left behind quite a legacy. They appeared in a total of 220 films. Since 1958 they've never been off television for very long. Decades after they made their last film, they are still popular all over the world. Even today people can buy Three Stooges barbecue sauce, beach towels, and action figures. Some TV channels still celebrate New Year's with day-long Three Stooges marathons. Many of their films are available on the Internet.

Even after all their success, the Three Stooges seemed to be the same boys they had been growing up in Brooklyn and Philadelphia. They wanted to make people—and each other—laugh. They have poked and bopped and nyuk-nyuked their way from the vaudeville stage to movies to television and the Internet.

Not bad for a bunch of Stooges.

Timeline of the Three Stooges' Life

1895	Samuel "Shemp" Horwitz is born
1897	Moses "Moe" Horwitz is born
1902	Larry Feinberg is born
1903	Jerome "Curly" Horwitz is born
1916	Shemp and Moe start a comedy act
1925	Shemp marries Gertrude Frank
	Moe marries Helen Schonberger
1926	Larry Fine marries Mabel Haney
1932	Curly Howard becomes a Stooge
1934	The Three Stooges sign a contract with Columbia Studios to make eight movies a year for twenty-five years
	Men in Black is nominated for an Academy Award
1939	The Three Stooges go to London
1946	Shemp joins the Three Stooges
1952	Curly Howard dies
1955	Shemp Howard dies
1956	Joe Besser joins the Stooges as "Joe"
1958	Joe DeRita joins the Stooges as "Curly Joe"
1975	Larry Fine dies
	Moe Howard dies

Timeline of the World

1895	The X-ray is discovered
1897	The *New York Sun* runs "Yes, Virginia, There Is a Santa Claus" editorial
1900	Kodak introduces the "Brownie" camera
1905	Earthquake in Kangra, India, kills twenty thousand
1912	The Dixie cup is patented
1919	Storage tank of molasses bursts, and a flood of molasses kills twenty-one and injures 150 in Boston, Massachusetts
1924	Ice cream cone rolling machine, invented in Cleveland, is patented
1933	The movie *King Kong* opens
1948	Earthquake hits Fukui, Japan
1958	British Overseas Airways Corporation flies first transatlantic passenger jet trip from New York to Paris
1965	United States announces it will send forces to fight in Vietnam
1967	The Six-Day War is fought between Israel and its Arab neighbors
1974	The game Dungeons & Dragons is released in the United States

Bibliography

Feinberg, Morris. ***My Brother Larry: The Stooge in the Middle***. San Francisco: Last Gasp of San Francisco, 1984.

Gallagher, Danny. "Ten Things You Didn't Know About the Three Stooges, ***ScreenCrush***, April 3, 2012. http://screencrush.com/didnt-know-about-three-stooges/

Howard, Moe. ***I Stooged to Conquer***. Chicago: Chicago Review Press, 2013.

Lenburg, Jeff, Greg Lenburg, and Joan Howard Maurer. ***The Three Stooges Scrapbook***. Chicago: Chicago Review Press, 1982.

Maurer, Joan Howard. ***Curly: An Illustrated Biography of the Superstooge***. Chicago: Chicago Review Press, 2013.

Roberts, Jeremy. "Paul Howard, Son of Moe, Remembers Growing Up with the Three Stooges." ***Examiner.com***, July 27, 2011. http://www.examiner.com/article/paul-howard-son-of-moe-remembers-growing-up-with-the-three-stooges

The Three Stooges Official Website: www.threestooges.com/